WHEN MY MOMMY DIED

a child's view of death

by Janice M. Hammond, Ph.D.

WHEN MY MOMMY DIED
is an original publication of Cranbrook Publishing Co..
This work has never appeared in book form.

CRANBROOK PUBLISHING COMPANY
2815 Cranbrook Drive
Ann Arbor, Michigan 48104

Copyright ©1980 by Janice M. Hammond

ISBN: 0-9604690-0-1

Printed in the U.S.A.

IDEAS FOR USING THIS BOOK

Read the book with the child.

Let the child stop and talk about the character in the story.
Ask, "When did you ever feel that way."
Share your own feelings about death.
Do not force the child to talk if they do not want to.
At a later time the child may want to read the book again and talk.
The child may want to color the pictures while talking.
You can use the final pages for the child to write and illustrate his or her own story too.
Don't expect your child to come to accept death as quickly as the child in the book did.
Grief takes time.

The death of a parent may be the most difficult event in a person's life.
It is hoped that this book will help children learn that the many different feelings they may be having are O.K.
The simple pictures and sentences encourage children to add their own thoughts to the story.

The book is meant to be read and talked about with a caring adult.

JANICE M. HAMMOND has a Doctorate in Elementary School Counseling from The University of Michigan. She has worked as an elementary school teacher, reading specialist, elementary school counselor, and has taught counseling classes to university students. Dr. Hammond has conducted many workshops for parents and educators on the topic of helping children cope with loss through death and divorce.

For Jason and Jennifer,
whose Mommy died

Preface for Adults

A death in the family is always a painful experience. Especially tragic is the death of a young parent. The remaining spouse, involved in his or her own grief, as well as in the many arrangements and readjustments, may find it difficult to be available and helpful to the child. Yet the child's need for the parent during this time will perhaps never be greater.

Often the initial response of adults is to protect and shelter children from grief and the reality of death. It is sometimes thought that the children will not understand. Yet experts tell us that even a child of two can be helped to comprehend and feel saddened by the loss of a parent. Psychiatrists emphasize that if a death is not accepted and grief worked through in childhood a number of behavioral and emotional problems may arise later.

Although accepting the death of a loved one is difficult for all of us, children have some unique needs:

- While adults invest their love in a number of people (spouse, parents, children, friends, and even their work), children have given the vast majority of their love and caring to their parents; and therefore have so much to loose when a parent dies. Never at any time in life can a person be hurt as deeply as when a child's parent dies.

- Children are dependent on parents in many ways. When a parent dies, the children may wonder and fear that no one will take care of them in the special way the parent did.

- Children may have angry feelings toward the parent who died. They may blame the parent's death for the changes they do not like in their home situation. They may feel it is not fair that other children have both a mother and a father. At the same time a child may feel guilty for having the angry feeling.

- Children may feel guilty and believe their behavior, in some way, caused their parent's death. They may think, for example, that being naughty or noisy caused a parent to become ill.

- Some of the common messages given to children about death may be frightening. Telling children that death is just like sleeping may make them afraid to go to sleep for fear that they will never wake up. One child was told, "Your Mother will always be with you." He was frightened that he might reach out in the dark and touch her body.

- Children will model their response to death after the other adults in the family. Therefore if there is no discussion of the person who died, or no sorrow expressed, the children will believe they should keep their thoughts to themselves, too.

- Children often believe that if they wish for something it may come true. It would be common for a child, in an angry mood, to have wished that the parent was dead. Therefore they may think they caused the death by wishing for it.

The aspect of death the child is most concerned with often depen-depends on his or her age:

- Ages 1-4 -- The child is mainly concerned with meeting his or her physical needs. At this age it is hard for the child to understand things not seen. It is very important for the child to be cared for by an adult he or she can come to depend on.
- Ages 4-7 -- The biological process of death is being discovered. Questions will tend to be factual. Again, there will be concern over who will care for them.
- Ages 7-above -- The child's main concern is that a close relationship has been lost. Discussion will help the child readjust.

WHAT CAN ADULTS DO TO HELP THE CHILD?

1) As soon as possible after the death, set aside time to gently, yet truthfully, tell the child about it. Choosing a familiar room or outdoor setting to talk may help the child feel more comfortable.

2) Be truthful. Do not make up stories that will have to be changed later. If no one will answer a child's questions he or she may imagine the parent's death to be far more terrifying that it was. Even the knowledge that the parent died as a result of a homicide, suicide, or violent accident is usually best shared with the child.

3) Do not burden the child with information he or she is not ready for. Children need a logical explanation of why a person died, but they may not want all of the details for days or weeks afterwards. Be sensitive to what information the child is asking for.

4) Encourage the child to express feelings. Share your own feelings. Don't be afraid to cry in their presence. Cry together; hold each other.

5) Take the children to the funeral. Let them observe others mourning. Older children may feel useful by comforting an adult with a hug or holding a hand, helping with visitors, serving dinners, and being included in some decisions about the funeral.

6) If the parent is to be buried, it will be helpful for the children to be present so they will know where the body is and where they may return to visit.

7) Let the children tell others that their parent has died if they wish. The subject should be as open and comfortable as possible, rather than something that is hidden.

8) In the weeks and months following the death talk about the missing parent. Casually mention things the parent said or did. Recall funny stories, happy, and unhappy incidents together. Encourage the child to talk about the things he or she remembers, too.

9) Let the child know you are available to answer any question. Show that you believe anger, sorrow, loneliness, and fear are all right to feel, and that you will be glad to talk about each concern as it arises.

10) When we share difficult feelings people try to be helpful by saying, "You shouldn't feel that way." What we need is to have our emotions accepted. Examples of accepting the child's feelings are: "You're really feeling angry that Susie has a mommy and you don't;" or "It seems like you're scared that your Daddy might die too."

Most of all just be yourself. Accept and talk about what you are feeling, and your children will be encouraged, by your example, to do the same. Through sharing grief, your family's closeness may increase to a depth never imagined. Often through crisis comes growth.

Daddy took me for a long walk.
He said Mommy won't be with us anymore.
He said she died.

Daddy said that dying is a hard thing for even grown-ups to understand.

I went to the funeral. There were lots of flowers and lots of people. Some of the people were crying. My Grandma cried and cried. My Daddy cried and cried. I cried too.

I was a little scared to look in the casket.
It looked like my Mom was just sleeping.

I remember when I had two goldfish.
One day they would not move.
I told Daddy they were just sleeping.
Daddy said he was sorry but they were dead.
I cried and cried.

I buried them in the back yard.

I wish Mommy was just sleeping and would wake up and be with me again.

But I know when people die they can never come back.

Sometimes now I forget that Mommy died.
I think about what I will tell her when I get home.

But then I remember and feel sad again.

Sometimes I worry about who will take care of me.

Daddy says that he loves me, and will see that I am always taken care of.

Sometimes I worry that Daddy feels so sad that he might die. Sometimes I think about me dying too.

Daddy says that most people live for a long, long time until they are very old. He thinks we will live to be very old grandmas and grandpas.

Sometimes I get angry at my Mom for dying and leaving me.

Sometimes I just want to scream,
"I want my Mommy back."

Daddy says it's O.K. for me

to talk about Mommy,

and cry,

and even scream sometimes.

He says that it is good to let my feelings out and not keep them inside of me.

I used to think if I had been very good and helped Mommy more she wouldn't have died. I know now that isn't so. I couldn't have done anything to keep her from dying.

It wasn't my fault.

Everyday I feel a little bit better.
We moved to a new house and I have lots of friends.
School keeps me busy too.

I still feel sad sometimes when I miss Mommy, but I know that's O.K. I know I can be happy and have lots of fun with my friends and family and school.

Someday Daddy might marry someone nice and I would have a new mother.

I think I would like that.
But I will always remember my Mommy too.

Man y people have been nice to me. We do a lot of
fun things together.

But best of all I have my Daddy.
We talk together and help each other even more now.
I know he loves me and I love him so much too.

Would you like to write your own story?

When my Mommy died I felt _____

Sometimes I worry about _____

These are some things I remember about my Mommy_____

Some things I enjoy are _____

Now I'm feeling _____

Now that I've finished the book, here are some things that I learned _____

OTHER BOOKS FOR CHILDREN ABOUT DEATH

Andres, Rebecca, A LOOK AT DEATH (Minniapolis, Minn.: The Lerner Awareness Books, 1977)

   For Grades 3-6.

Bernstein, Joanne and Gullo, Stephen, WHEN PEOPLE DIE (New York: Dutton, 1977)

   Explains in simple terms theories on afterlife, burial practices, grief, and the naturalness of death in the chain of life. Grades 1-6.

Brown, M., THE DEAD BIRD (Reading, Mass.: Addison-Wesley, 1958)

   A beautiful story for elementary school children.

Fassler, Joan, MY GRANDPA DIED TODAY (New York: Human Sciences Press, 1971)

   The lovely story of a young boy's adjustment to his grandfather's death.
   This picture book is appealing to all ages.

LeShan, Eda, LEARNING TO SAY GOODBYE: WHEN A PARENT DIES (New York:MacMillian, 1976)

   Non-fiction. An excellent, sensitive book for grades 5 through high school.

Mann, Peggy, THERE ARE TWO KINDS OF TERRIBLE (New York: Doubleday, 1977)

   Fiction for middle school students. Peggy Mann writes in a style that is especially appealing to pre-adolescents.

Smith, Doris, A TASTE OF BLACKBERRIES (New York: T.Y. Crowell, 1973)

   The beautiful story of a young boy's acceptance of his best friend's death. Grades 4-8.

Viorst, Judith, THE TENTH GOOD THING ABOUT BARNEY (New York: Atheneum Publications, 1975)

   A sensitive picture book about the death and burial of the children's cat. Grades K-4.

BOOKS FOR ADULTS ABOUT CHILDREN AND DEATH

Furman, Erma, A CHILD'S PARENT DIES (New Haven, Conn.:Yale University Press, 1974)

Psychiatrists accounts of case studies of children who have had a parent die.

Grollman, Earl, TALKING ABOUT DEATH (Boston: Beacon Press, 1970)

Grollman, Earl A., ed. EXPLAINING DEATH TO CHILDREN (Boston: Beacon Press, 1967)

Chapters written by clergy and others.

Gordon, Audrey and Klass, Dennis THEY NEED TO KNOW, HOW TO TEACH CHILDREN ABOUT DEATH (Englewood Cliffs, New Jersey: Prentice-Hall, 1979)

An excellent resource for parents, educators, and social workers.

Tessman, Lara Heims, CHILDREN OF PARTING PARENTS (New York: Jason Aronson, Inc., 1978)

Accounts of psychotheraphy with children who have lost a parent through death or divorce.

Books to help kids cope

PRICES
(for any combination of books)

quantity	unit	cost	handling	total
1	3.95	3.95*	1.00	4.95
5	3.70	18.50*	1.50	20.00
10	3.25	32.50*	2.00	34.50
25	2.75	68.75*	3.25	72.00

*Michigan residents add 4% sales tax.

ORDER FORM

Make checks payable and send to:
Cranbrook Publishing Company
2815 Cranbrook
Ann Arbor, Michigan 48104

Please send me: _____copies of <u>When My Mommy Died: A Child's View of Death</u>

_____copies of <u>When My Dad Died</u>

_____copies of <u>Group Counseling for Children of Divorce</u>

_____copies of <u>Divorce Group Counseling for Secondary School Students</u>

Total _____ Enclosed is a check or purchase order for $_____

Name_____ Organization_____

Address_____

_____ Zip _____